I'm Reading About

FLORIDA

The Sunshine State!

GALLOPADE

by Carole Marsh

Printed and Manufactured in Peachtree City, GA., USA
www.gallopade.com

Book design: John Hanson

Editorial manager: Janice Baker

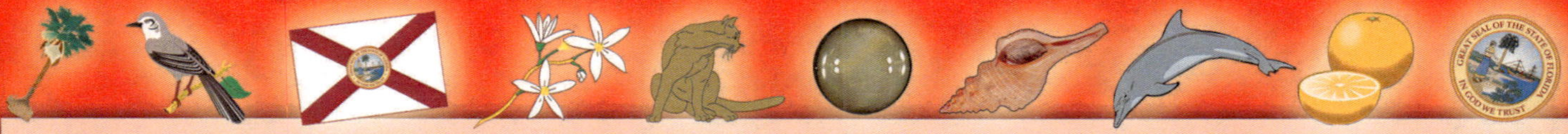

Florida is a great state.
It is one of a kind.

What makes Florida special?
Let's read about it
and see!

NATIVE AMERICANS

Who lived in Florida first?

Native Americans did!

They moved around to find food.
They hunted in Florida's woods.
They fished in Florida's rivers.
They gathered fruits and seeds and nuts.

EXPLORERS

The first explorers came to Florida in 1513.
They came from the country of Spain.

Juan Ponce de León was their leader.
He and his men were looking for
the Fountain of Youth!

SETTLEMENT

Settlers came from Spain to America.
They started the first settlement in Florida.
They named it St. Augustine.

St. Augustine is the oldest settlement in the United States!

St. Augustine

STATEHOOD

Florida was the 27th state
to join the United States of America!

Isn't it great,
to be a state!
I bet Florida
could hardly wait!

Florida became a state in 1845.

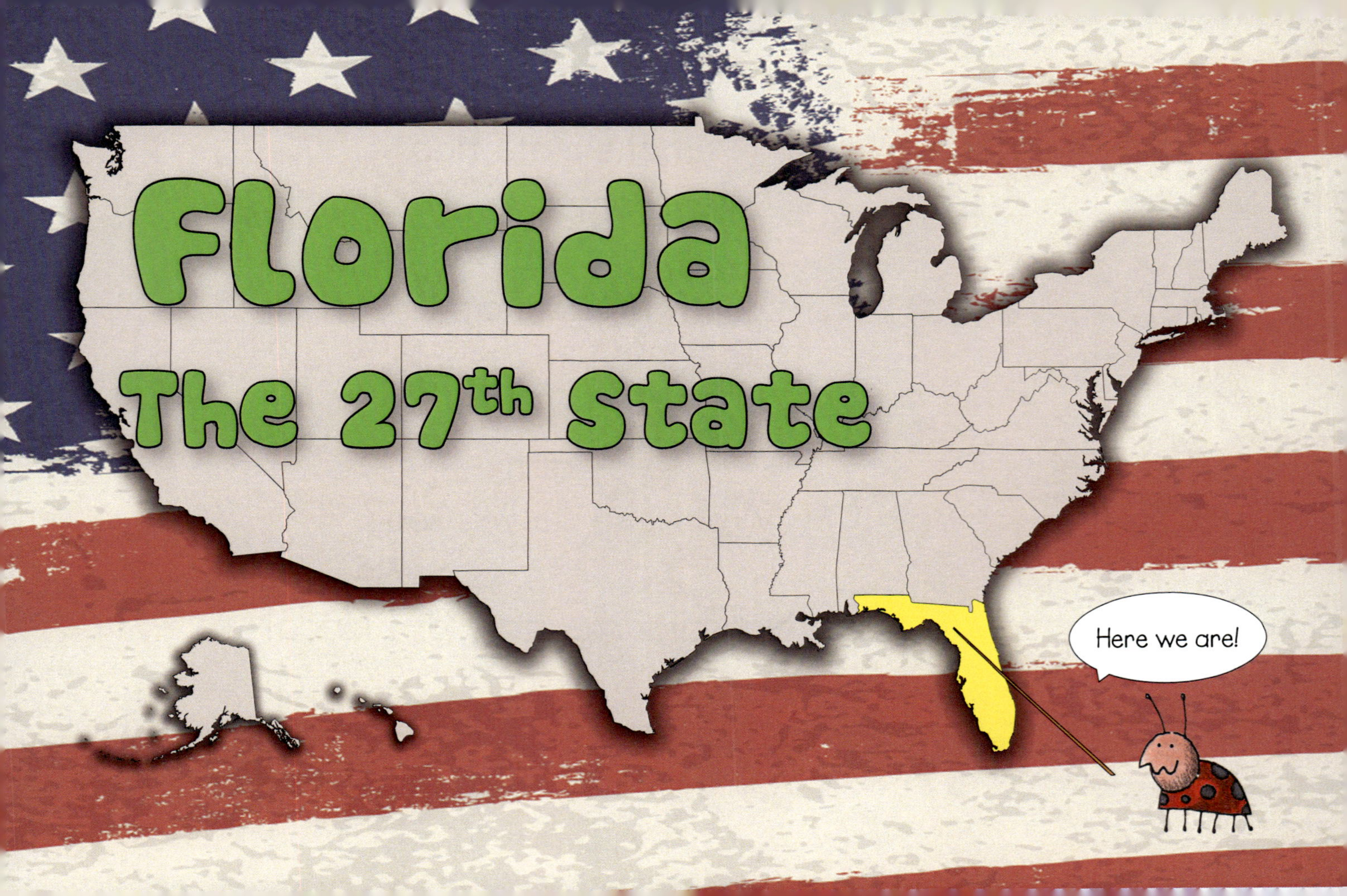
Florida
The 27th State
Here we are!

FLAG

I am the state flag.
I was adopted in 1900.

What colors am I?
Red. White. Gold.

Look at me.
What else do you see?

I fly high over the state of Florida!

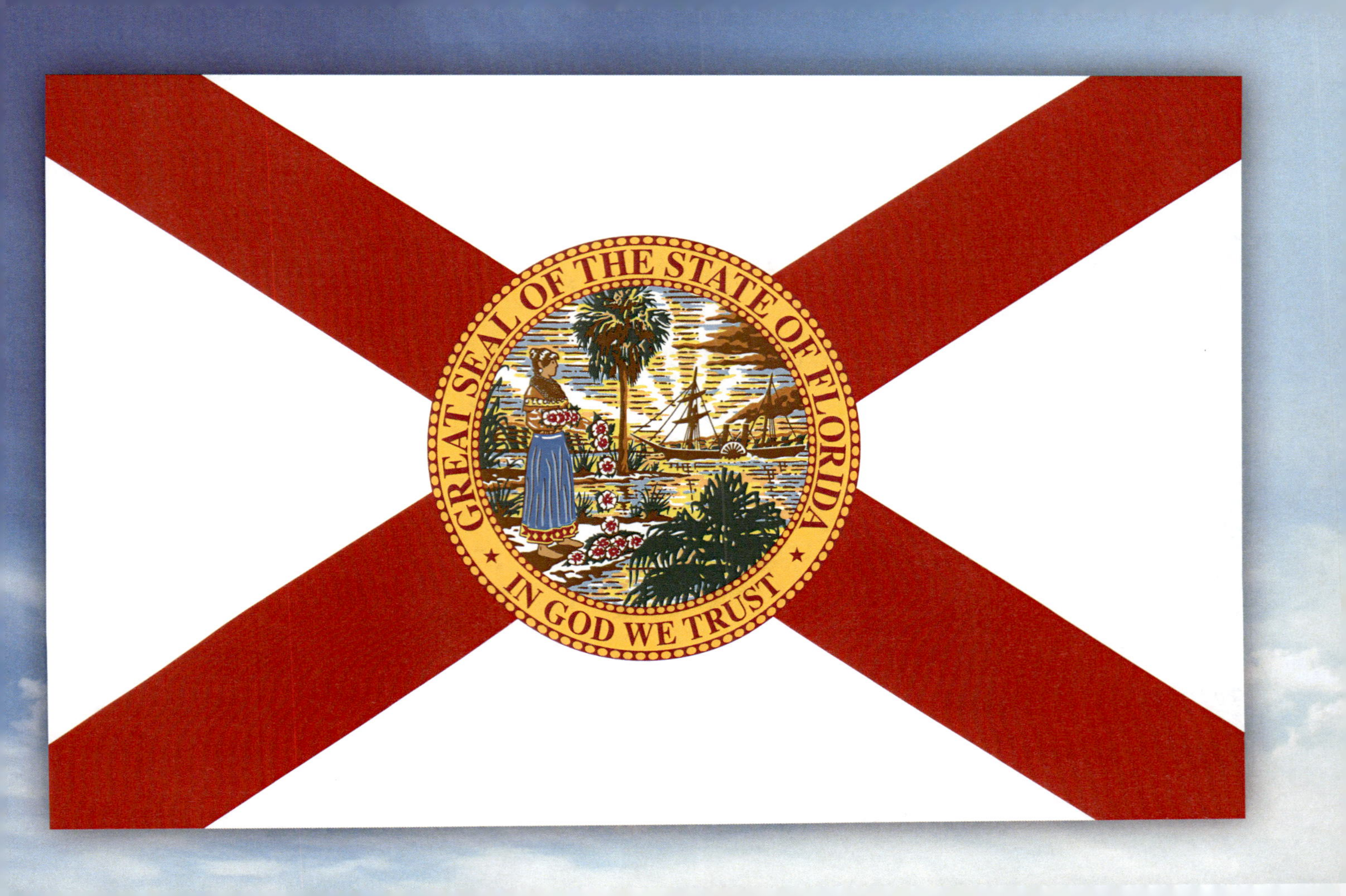
GREAT SEAL OF THE STATE OF FLORIDA
IN GOD WE TRUST

CAPITAL

Say hello to Tallahassee,
the capital city of Florida!

There is an important building in Tallahassee.
It is the State Capitol.
Florida's laws are made there!

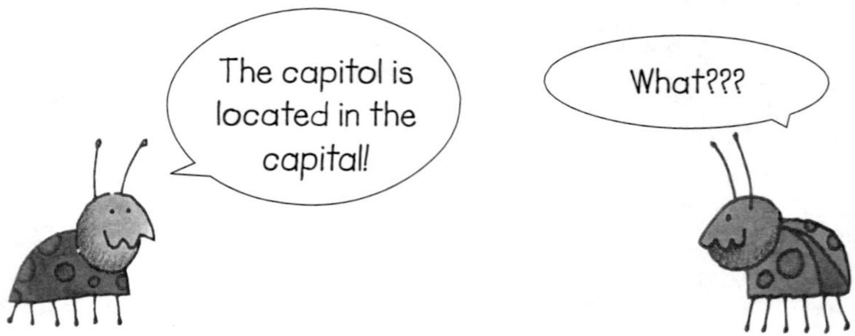

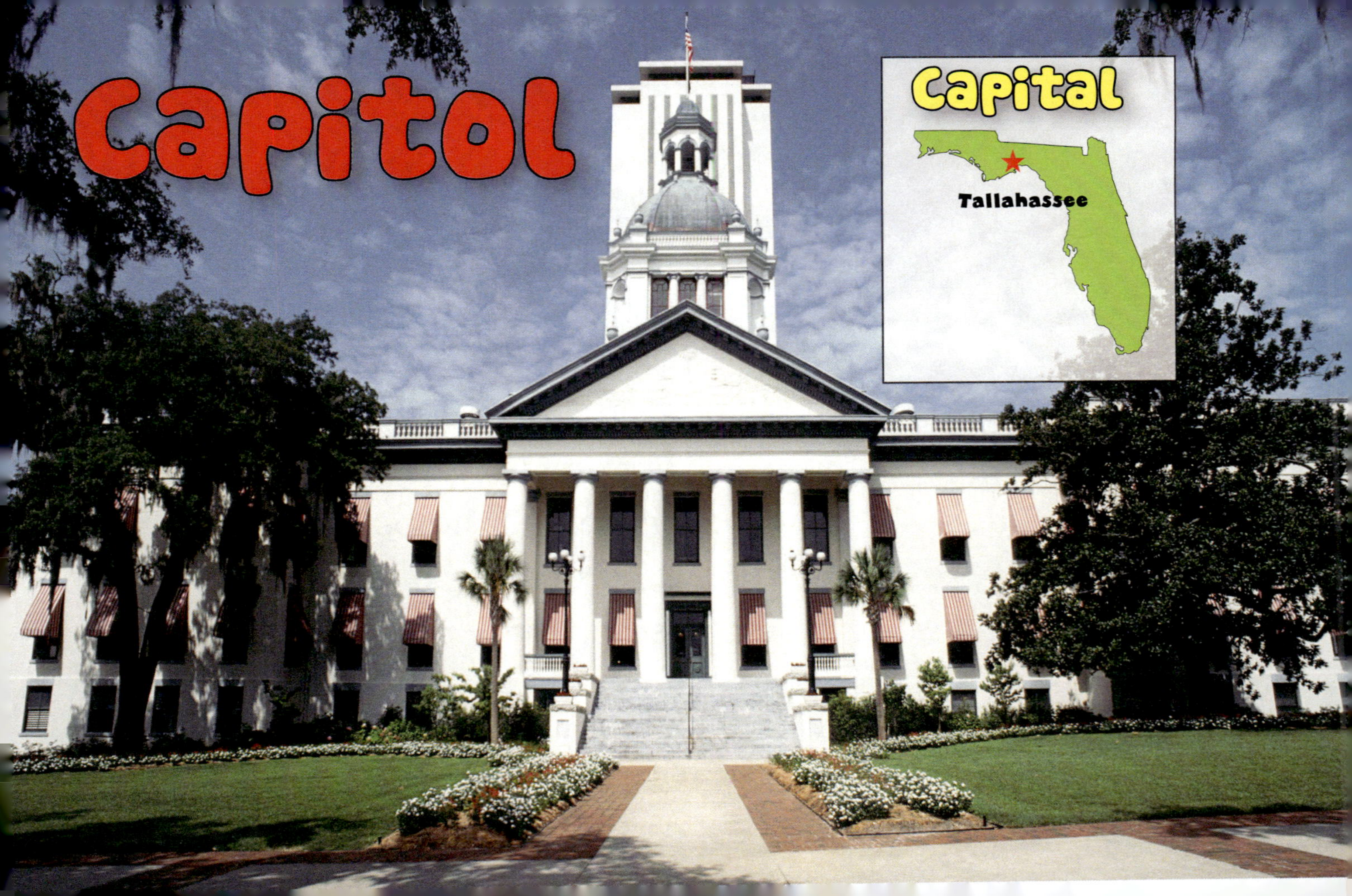
Capitol
Capital
Tallahassee

SEAL

I am a seal,
but I am not the State Seal.
If I were, I would be very important.
I would be stamped on many official papers.
(Ouch, that might hurt!)

GREAT SEAL OF THE STATE OF FLORIDA
IN GOD WE TRUST

Now, that's official!

NICKNAME

State nicknames are fun!
State nicknames are great!
They share fun facts
about each state!

Florida's nickname is "The Sunshine State."

Florida has lots of sunny days!

The Sunshine State

BORDERS

Look at Florida.
Florida is in a region called "the South."

Florida borders two other states.
Find them on the map!

Florida means "flowery land."

Borders

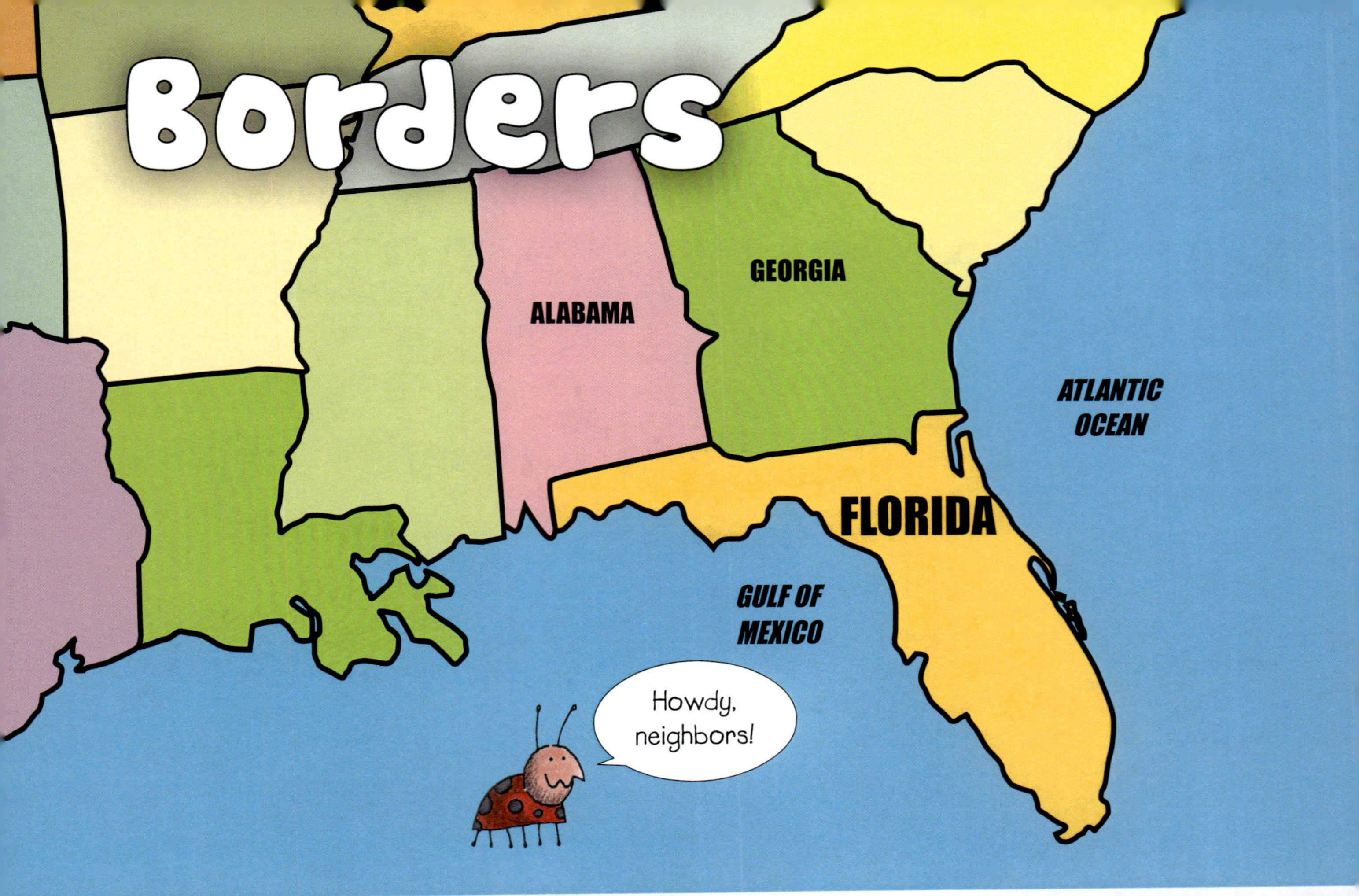
GEORGIA
ALABAMA
FLORIDA
ATLANTIC OCEAN
GULF OF MEXICO
Howdy, neighbors!

COUNTIES

Florida is divided into 67 counties.
Counties are a form of local government.
Counties provide services that people need!

Those services include:

Schools **Parks** **Libraries** **Police**
Firefighters **and More!**

Counties

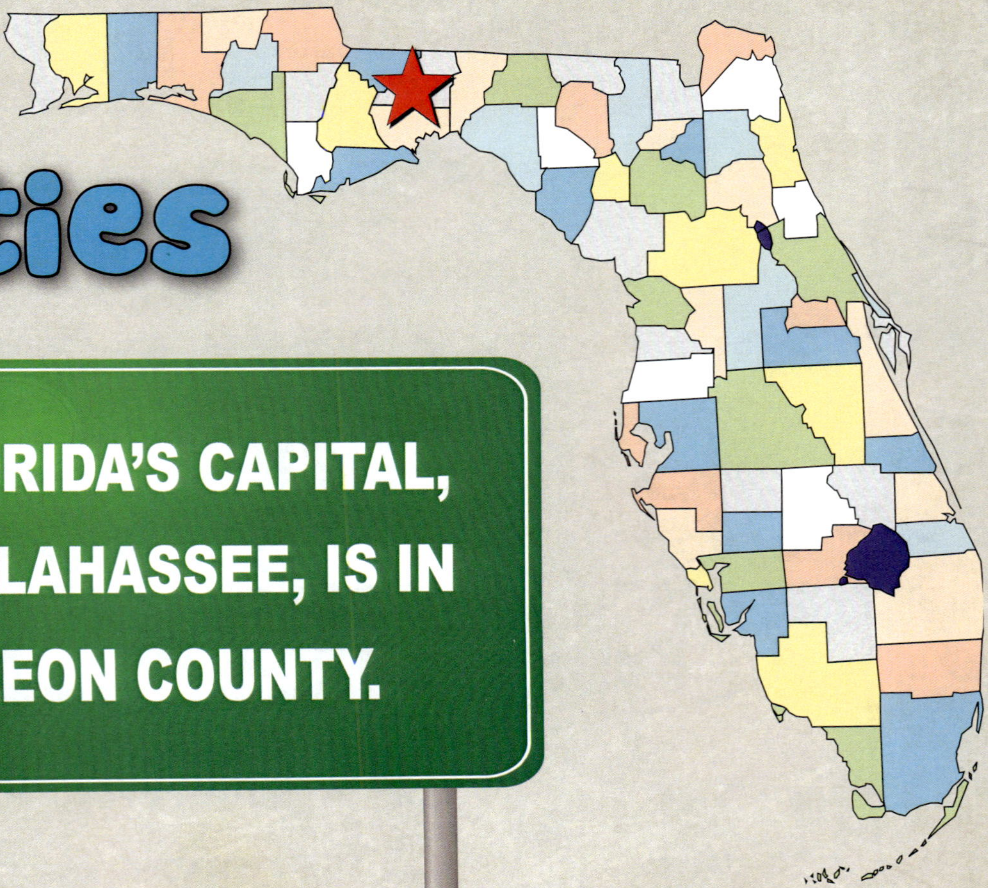

FLORIDA'S CAPITAL, TALLAHASSEE, IS IN LEON COUNTY.

PEOPLE

Many famous people

Osceola

Leader of the Seminole Indians

Henry Flagler

Built railroad that led to Florida's growth

Jacqueline Cochran

Pilot who led the training of female pilots during World War II

call our state home!

Ray Charles
Blind musician known as "The Father of Soul Music"

Wallace Amos
Founder of Famous Amos Chocolate Chip Cookies

Janet Reno
First female Attorney General of the U.S.

PEOPLE

Mockingbird

BIRD

I am the state bird, and I fly
over Florida, proud and high.

As I fly, up in the sky,
I flap my wings to tell you "Hi!"

The Florida state bird is the Mockingbird.

Orange Blossom

FLOWER

I am the Orange Blossom.
I am the state flower.

I grow where it's warm and sunny.
I bloom in early spring.
I help make Florida beautiful!

Look at me! Smell me!
I grow on the orange tree!

Sabal Palm

TREE

I am a Sabal Palm—I'm the state tree.
Along the coast is where to find me.

My roots run deep, they keep me strong.
My leaves can be several feet long.

I stand up straight, big and tall.
Don't climb too high—it would hurt to fall!

Zebra Longwing Butterfly

BUTTERFLY

I am the Zebra Longwing Butterfly.
I am the state butterfly.

I flit and I fly from flower to flower.
I am looking for nectar to drink.

Look at my beautiful wings.
What colors do you see?

Beaches

BEACHES

Lets go to the beach!

We can swim in the waves.
We can play in the sand.

We can build a big castle
where water meets land.

Florida's beaches are home to many animals:

Sea Turtles **Fish** **Birds** **Crabs** **Dolphins** **and More!**

Lakes

Lets go to the lake!

We can wade in the water.
We can ride on a boat.

We can jump off the dock
onto an inner tube float!

Everglades

SWAMPS

There are several swamps in Florida.
The best-known swamp is in south Florida.
It is called the Everglades.

This habitat is home to many animals:

Birds Deer Snakes Frogs Alligators and More!

More than 200,000 alligators live in the Everglades!

Kennedy Space Center

LANDMARK

The Kennedy Space Center is in Florida.

Rockets are launched into space there.
A rocket launch is very exciting to watch!

The Vehicle Assembly Building is one of the largest buildings in the world!

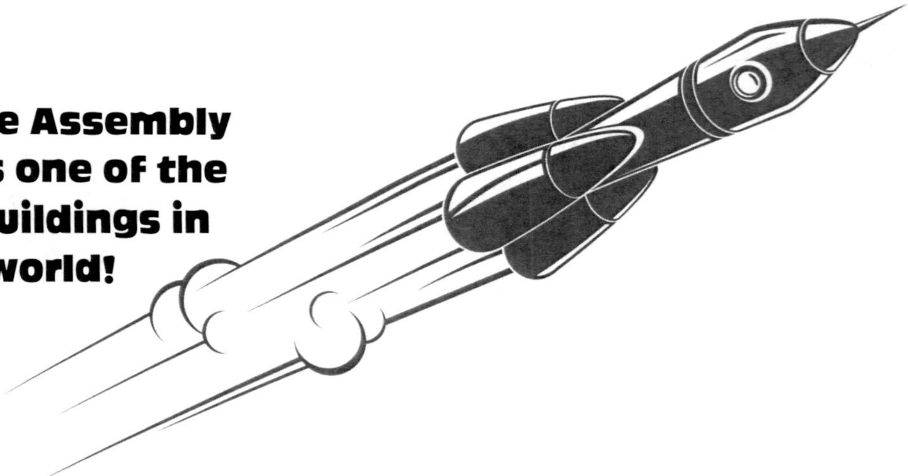

Florida Crops

AGRICULTURE

Florida has many farms.
Why?
Because Florida has good soil and a warm climate!

Some of the top crops grown in Florida are:

Oranges **Grapefruit**

Sugarcane **Potatoes**

Sports in Florida

SPORTS

Baseball! Basketball! Football!
Florida has it all.

Whether you like to watch or play,
You are sure to have a ball!

Marlins **Rays** **Heat**

Magic **Jaguars** **Dolphins**

Buccaneers **Gators**

Seminoles

& More!

Florida: Home of Walt Disney World

CLAIM TO FAME

Walt Disney World is a huge theme park!
People from all over the world visit the park.
It is the most popular tourist attraction in Florida.

Walt Disney kept his idea
for Disney World a secret.
He bought all the land
without anyone knowing!

GLOSSARY

Attorney General: the chief law officer of a nation or state

climate: weather conditions in an area over a long period of time

habitat: a place where plants or animals naturally live

laws: rules made by the government

musician: someone who performs music

popular: liked, admired, or enjoyed by many people

region: an area that has similar characteristics

settlement: the first community in an area

swamp: a low area of land that is often partly covered with water

theme park: an amusement park where all the settings and attractions are centered around one subject